Facts About the Caracal

By Lisa Strattin

© 2016 Lisa Strattin

Revised © 2020

FREE BOOK

FOR ALL SUBSCRIBERS

LisaStrattin.com/Subscribe-Here

BOX SET

Get Yours Here

LisaStrattin.com/BookBundle

Facts for Kids Picture Books by Lisa Strattin

Pygmy Rabbit, Vol 153

Jumping Rabbit, Vol 154

Mini Rabbits, Vol 155

Blue Quail, Vol 156

Mountain Quail, Vol 157

Quokka, Vol 158

Quoll, Vol 159

Raccoon, Vol 160

Raccoon Dog, Vol 161

Radiated Tortoise, Vol 162

Sign Up for New Release Emails Here

http://LisaStrattin.com/subscribe-here

Contents

INTRODUCTION

The caracal is also commonly known as the Persian Lynx or African Lynx, despite the fact that the caracal is not a lynx at all. The caracal is thought to be most closely related to the African golden cat and the serval.

The caracals name is believed to come from the Turkish word Karakulak, which means black ears.

It possesses tremendous speed and agility, the caracal is a strong predator capable of tackling prey two to three times its size. Its long, powerful hind legs enable it to make incredible leaps up to three metres high and catch birds in flight by batting them from the air with its large paws.

In the past, this ability led to many caracals being trained to hunt game birds for the Indian royalty. The caracal is also the fastest cat of its size, and uses its speed to run down prey such as hyraxes, hares and small antelopes. This species is superbly adapted for life in arid environments and requires very little water, apparently getting adequate supplies from its food.

CHARACTERISTICS

The caracal is a slender, moderately sized cat characterized by tufted ears, black on the back, long canine teeth, a short face, long legs and a robust build. It reaches nearly 40–50 centimeters tall (16–20 in) at the shoulder; the head-and-body length is typically 78 centimeters (31 in) for males and 73 centimeters (29 in) for females. While males weigh 12–18 kilograms (26–40 lb), females weigh 8–13 kilograms (18–29 lb). The tan, bushy tail measures 26–34 centimeters (10–13 in), and extends to the hocks.

Caracals are very difficult to see in the wild as they are able to hide themselves extremely well.

Caracals have brown to red coats, with color varying among individuals. Females are typically lighter than males. Their undersides are white and, similar to African golden cats, have many small spots. The face has black markings on the whisker pads, around the eyes, above the eyes and faintly down the center of the head and nose.

The trademark features of caracals are their elongated and black-tufted ears. The legs are relatively long and the hind legs are disproportionately tall and well-muscled. The tail is short. Eye color varies from golden or copper to green or grey. Juveniles differ in their shorter ear tufts and blue tinted eyes.

Subspecies of Caracal may not be easily distinguishable. Although the tail is short, it still makes up a significant portion of the total body length. Tail length ranges from 18 cm (7 in) to 34 cm (13 in). Head and body length is measured from the nose to the base of the tail and ranges from 62 to 91 cm (about 24 to 36 in). Even the smallest adult caracal is larger than most domestic cats.

LIFE SPAN

Caracals can live about 20 years in captivity.

SIZE

The caracal is famous in Iran and India for bird hunting. As the name implies, the backs of the ears are black and tufted with long black tufts about 4.5 centimeters long. This long black tuft is the characteristic that Caracals do share with their lynx family members. It is the largest member of Africa's small cats, and it's most formidable.

Males usually weigh as much as 40 pounds, and females as much as 35 pounds.

HABITAT

The wild cats live in the drier savannah and woodland regions of sub-Saharan Africa. They prefer the more scrubby, arid habitats. They will also inhabit evergreen forests, but are not found in tropical rain forests.

DIET

Caracals relies on a number of mammals for food, with the most common being rodents, hares, gazelles, rabbits, hyraxes, and small antelope. Unlike other small African cats, they do not even try to kill prey larger then themselves. They store their kills in trees, just like leopards. Although these wild cats are mostly nocturnal, they have been found during daylight hours in protected areas. Caracals at the San Diego Zoo are fed a fortified meat-based commercial carnivore diet as their staple diet, along with cat kibble, while fish and mouse might be offered once a week as a special treat.

ENEMIES

Wolves are the natural enemy of Caracal.

SUITABILITY AS PETS

There are few things to consider before considering the caracal as a pet. Check your local laws to make sure you can have one as a pet. The most suitable place for caracal is a home with a field or acreage where the cat can roam and exercise.

Although, they can be trained easily to walk on a leash like a dog, they need raw meat and high-quality dry food in their diet. And because they can jump very high, you must have a tall fence to keep them from getting out.

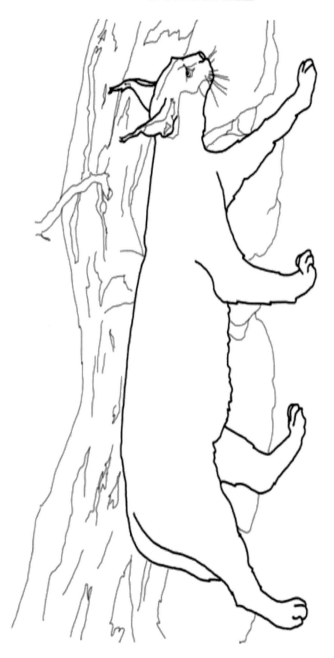

COLOR ME

COLOR ME

COLOR ME

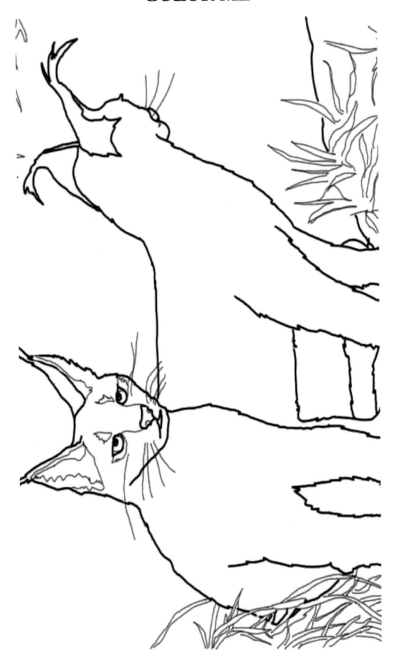

Please leave me a review here:

http://lisastrattin.com/Review-Vol-21

For more Kindle Downloads Visit Lisa Strattin Author Page on Amazon Author Central

http://amazon.com/author/lisastrattin

To see upcoming titles, visit my website at LisaStrattin.com– all books available on kindle!

http://lisastrattin.com

FREE BOOK

FOR ALL SUBSCRIBERS

LisaStrattin.com/Subscribe-Here

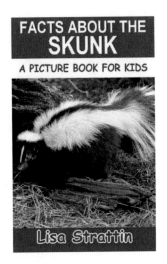

LisaStrattin.com/Facebook

LisaStrattin.com/Youtube

Made in the USA
Middletown, DE
07 December 2020